Choice and Structure for Children with Autism

Second Edition

Colette McNeil

Copyright 2022
MSI Press LLC
1760 Airline Hwy, #203
Hollister, CA 95023

All rights reserved. No part of this book may be reproduced or utilized in any form or by any means, digital or mechanical, including photocopying, recording, or by any information and retrieval system, without permission in writing from the publisher.

Copyeditor: Mary Ann Raemisch

Book design: Opeyemi Ikuborije

ISBN: 9781957354187

LCCN: 2022917275

CONTENTS

Acknowledgements. 1

Introduction. 3

Choice 7

Satiation and Fixation 25

Environmental Structure 35

The Dance 45

Comprehension and Communication 59

Conclusion. 75

References 81

About this Book. 83

About the Author. 91

Related MSI Press Books 97

Letter to the Reader 99

Acknowledgements

I would like to thank my family for their undying support and ever-present encouragement! This book would not be the same had I not the grace of their care.

I would like to thank all the children and their families that have blessed me with the opportunity to learn all that I share within these pages. I thank my fellow special education educators who have influenced my path along the way.

I would like to recognize the community of psychologists, counselors, coaches, and fellow seekers of harmony who encourage, teach and write about positive psychology, communication, relationships, and understanding of the human condition. Among this assembly, I thank the community of Choice Theory practitioners who follow and expand on the teachings of Dr. William Glasser M.D. Your ideas inspire me and spark my own. I have been forever changed for the better for having known you.

CHAPTER 1

Introduction

Choice & Structure for Children with Autism is about identifying and celebrating the role of structure in supporting autistic children. We want children with autism to do more than exist—not just live, but confidently engage in home life. We desire for them to do more than survive. We hold out hope that they grow to the best of their individual potentials. Research and experience have shown autism advocates that structure is a great tool to that end. Children with autism absolutely thrive within high levels of structure. In the following chapters, I hope to show how that structure does not need to be rigid, overbearing, or difficult.

Many Long Days at Home

Our regular routines of school and work during the week and predictable weekend activities help all of us maintain balance. We know the schedule, we plan for the expectations, and we live these routines comfortably. What happens when these routines are disrupted? How do we and our children manage when weekends extend beyond Saturday and Sunday, or vacation days break the certainty in our activities?

Many long days of free play at home during weekends, holidays, school vacations and health quarantines can become challenging for children and their parents. All the toys have been played with, all the movies watched, and the overindulgence of home-bound activities has driven children to lose interest in the things around them. Toys, games, movies, and crafts are everywhere but kids complain that they are bored, quickly get into squabbles with their siblings and argue more with their parents.

Children with autism are no exception. Unfortunately, though, autistic children may express greater levels of frustration and stronger distressing emotions than their siblings and peers. Many children with autism typically have purposefully directed lives. Autistic children engage best in environments that are highly structured with predictable schedules and a high level of adult guidance. They spend their weekdays in school as do other children. And, they attend after school and weekend therapy, daily living skills instruction, behavioral services and specially designed recreational activities. It takes a variety of people with different knowledge bases to work with autistic children throughout the day. Due to their autism, these children already struggle with unstructured time and unpredictable situations. They easily become overwhelmed with too many things around them and a lack of direction. Long strings of days off schedule sets the stage for just the unstructured and unpredictable circumstances that are so challenging for children with autism.

After many hours of unstructured time, families may notice their children with autism distance themselves through heightened levels of self-stimulation (stim) behaviors. Autistic children may become more obsessive about keeping hold of particular toys or may become increasingly less-responsive to parent and sibling attempts at interaction. Toys may be played with briefly then discarded for another, and another, and another until the child becomes agitated. The child may choose to stim on one single toy, or have all their toys laid out across the floor not playing with anything. When approached or having requests made of them, children with autism may become quickly agitated or demanding, and express protest behaviors.

Often, without structure and predictability, autistic children will cycle through periods of isolation, self-stimulation and agitated engagement. Chaotic unsuccessful attempts of self-entertainment may be followed by making demands of parents, and tantrums. If this cycle is repeated daily it will become the new predictable routine: stim, seek entertainment, obsession, protest, melt down, stim, seek entertainment, obsession, protest, melt down etc... Many days in a row at this intensity could drain the best of us. When we add in the needs of the siblings, and stress of the parents, this situation could become exhausting very quickly. Difficult times often accompany long unstructured days at home. How can families improve upon this stressful prediction? How can they provide the supports needed to help children with autism stay emotionally well regulated, appropriately engaged, and cooperatively interactive with family members?

Some Simple Strategies

I would like to offer some simple strategies that could be helpful. Don't worry! I am not going to attempt to teach you how to make your home a strict Applied Behavioral Analysis (ABA) program. I simply hope to offer some ideas to organize your day and offer a better outcome than the dismal portrait described above. These strategies will assist parents in developing simple and safe routines and choices that will make long days at home more engaging, cooperative, and positively stimulating for children with autism, their parents and siblings.

Ideas that will help decrease boredom, protesting, and isolation, while increasing, engagement, interaction, and cooperation will be shared throughout this book. The chapters will have relatable life stories included. These stories will demonstrate the chapter topic and provide a foundation for a discussion of the information. In Chapter 2, an argument for creating plentiful opportunities for choice will be offered. These choice opportunities will be re-emphasized throughout each following chapter. In Chapter 3, the roles that satiation and fixation play in boredom and disengagement are explored. In Chapter 4, a look into enhancing environmental organization will be presented. In Chapter 5, a deep dive into the intricacies of choreographing the dance between space, energy and time will be embarked upon. In Chapter 6, a discussion focused on understanding and using predictable cues and visual supports will be provided. These supports will help children with autism to follow directions, communicate choices, and decrease anxiety. In chapter 7, the ideas throughout the previous chapters are revisited and summarized.

Showing how choice and structure can easily be included in the lives of families is my sincere endeavor.

CHAPTER 2

Choice

Providing an abundance of choice throughout the day can greatly improve the interactions between children with autism and their caregivers. Now, I can already hear your collective skepticism, "This is our home. Everything we have is free for the choosing. All the toys are out, all the snacks are free for the taking, every room and piece of furniture is the domain of the children. We offer *anything* to keep the peace! We are still struggling, and yet, you say that choice is the answer? Nonsense!"

Bear with me. *Please*! Yes, an abundance of choice is the answer with one little twist: *Structure*. Access to everything all the time is too much for a child with autism to process. Accepting that children with autism thrive on structure suggests that adults must help autistic children by structuring-up the choices. Give choice in everything the children do. And, identify only two to four choices per opportunity. *Structured choice* is the key.

Structured Choice

Presenting two to four choices to children multiple times throughout each activity will help them to be cooperative, focused and engaged. Further the presentation of choices gives children an opportunity to share their thoughts and interests helping them to feel worthwhile and significant. These feelings raise the level of a child's self-confidence. Self-confidence feels good, improving the child's mood and relationships. In the following sections, insights to the details of Structured Choice are provided. It may seem like quite-a-bit of information, yet once processed the act of utilizing Structure Choice is quick, easy and empowering for both children and adults.

How Many Choices to Offer?

Here are some tips for deciding how many choices to offer:

Two choices:

- Two choices are good during natural conversation where two options are easy and frequently offered.

- Two choices are good in a pinch where you are trying to influence cooperation or engagement with particular activities. Giving two choices when you can't quickly think of a third will, at minimum, give the child an opportunity to make a choice. Giving any opportunity to make a choice is better than no choice at all.

- Make your choice a "This or That" question. Do not make the choice a "yes or no" variety. Yes/No questions are too abstract or meaningless for many autistic children and may cause more harm than good. Abstract concepts are those with no physical form, action, or picture to attach meaning. These are very difficult for autistic children to understand. Further, yes/no questions open the door to an accept/refuse conflict that may prompt a power struggle. A "This or That" choice has a concrete form to see and is more productive. If deciding between "this or that" the child's focus is on accepting an offer. When focusing on accepting something there is a mental shift away from a want/don't-want power struggle. "This or That," is a choice that can be cooperatively achieved.

- Limit your words. When in a situation where you are only giving the choices through spoken instruction there is no item for the child to see. In this instance two choices may be the most information the child can process. Try to structure your spoken language so that the choice offered is only one or two words long. This will allow the autistic child plenty of head space to process the information heard. Ask your child questions such as, Do you choose to drink milk or juice? Would you like to paint or color?" The choices "Milk/Juice," or, "Paint/Color," can be repeated independently of the entire sentence. This repetition will act to highlight the important spoken information. Using your right and left hand to represent the choices may also help the child focus the subject on a physical spot. This provides 2 small pieces of spoken information, "Milk/Juice, or, Paint/Color," and a visual spot to imagine physically placing the items. As a result, communication and comprehension are assisted allowing the child to make a clear and quick choice.

Three choices:

- Three choices are ideal as it is not simply an either/or of the two-choice variety.
- Three choices are few enough so that decisions can be quickly made.
- Three choices are less likely to overwhelmed the child than larger numbers.
- Three Choices require visual supports: Visual supports are anything the child can see that helps provide information about the choices being offered. Visual supports are always a good idea when presenting information to children with autism. Even if just a single item is being offered such as showing a cup while asking, "do you want a drink?" a visual support helps. The more pieces of important information that is presented, the more essential visual supports become. Once three or more options are offered it becomes vital to use visual supports to aide in comprehension. These supports also assist in the ability respond and clearly communicate the desired selection. More information on visual supports will be presented in Chapter 6, Comprehension and Communication.

Four choices:

- Four choices can work if there is good reason for that many choices and visual supports are easily managed.
- It all depends on the circumstances:

- if the box of popsicles comes in four flavors then, ok, let the children pick from all four flavors.
- If all the other kids get to pick from four types of stickers then, ok, allow your child to pick from the same four.

- Remember, visual supports and limiting your words will be even more important with more choices.

Five or more choices:

Too many choices are counterproductive. Plenty of children struggle when the choices become too abundant because they can't focus on so much information at once. Children with autism are even more distracted by such high levels of information. Autistic children may take a long time deciding, or become overwhelmed by many choices and be unable to choose anything. Or, in a situation of free-for-all choices many children with autism will repeatedly only choose items on which they are fixated. Providing a smaller selection of choices during each opportunity and limiting access to fixation items will help the child to expand their engagement with other activities. Keep your choice options simple. Shoot for three choices as the norm and adjust down to two or up to four as the situation requires.

How to Offer a 3-Item Choice?

Here I offer you an example of how to walk through offering a 3-item choice using naturally occurring items.

- Present the item while speaking your offer: When asking a child to choose from 3 items such as milk, juice and water, if possible, hold or place all three items at equal distance apart.

- Ask, "would you like milk," (gesture toward or push forward the milk), "juice," (gesture to or push forward the juice), "or water?" (gesture toward or push forward the water)?"
- Pause a few seconds to allow the child to respond.
- If no response: Quickly repeat the offer a second time reducing your verbal language. Only speak the item name and repeat the indication of the item. "Milk, (gesture), Juice (gesture), Water (gesture)?"
- Here it is important to pause and wait for the child's response for at least 10 seconds.
- If no response, repeat the offer again using the reduced verbal language.
- Allow the child to make his/her preference known through whatever means is most independent.
- Immediately give the child the chosen item/activity!
- Voila you are done. See? Quick, easy, and empowering!

One Last Tip on Structured Choices

It is important to allow the child to respond and indicate their choice through whatever means the child is best able to communicate. If it is simply taking the preferred item, that's great! If it is pointing or words, that's awesome, too! While it is often good practice to teach new expressive communication skills throughout the normal activities of the day, be careful not to make every choice a challenging communication lesson. The choosing exchange itself is the focus here, not necessarily working on the child's speech and language goal. Practice these occasionally, yes, but if you spend too much time practicing new challenging speech and language skills, then your focus is in the wrong place. Structured Choice is not meant to frustrate and discourage children. If it is too hard to make choices, children will avoid doing so. Structured Choice is designed to be a quick and easy way to support children's cooperative interactions.

In Practice

Breakfast with Kiaan

Kiaan wanders sleepily into the kitchen and finds his mother standing at the stove. "Good morning, Kiaan," Mom engages her precious 7-year old. "Look, I am making omelets, I know you love omelets."

Kiaan turns away and goes to the cupboard to pull out some cereal. When he gets there, he finds a lock on the cupboard door. Over the past weeks of school vacation, Kiaan has developed a routine of pulling several boxes of cereal out of the cupboard and eating from them as he paces around the living room. This habit seemed to form quickly and has started to concern his mother. As Kiaan wanders the living room, he often drops pieces of cereal and smashes the food into a big mess while traipsing across the same area over and over. Further, Kiaan is eating from several boxes at a time, and he becomes anxious and quarrelsome if his siblings try to take a box for their own breakfast.

Kiaan's mother would prefer he and his siblings ate more of the healthy foods that she usually serves. During school days, Kiaan's mother regularly cooked breakfast for the family, and they ate sitting together at the table. Cereal was only served on the weekends to give Mom a break and support the sleep-in as late as you wish Saturday schedule. Now that the kids are staying home from school, every day has become Saturday, and Mom realizes that she is not happy with the habits the family is developing. So, this Monday morning Mom is determined to set the routine back to normal at least as far as meals are concerned.

Kiaan pulls Mom by the hand as a way of asking her to open the door so he can get the cereal. Mom discusses the locked cupboard with Kiaan, then says, "Today is Monday, and we are eating omelets for breakfast, come see what we have."

Kiaan doesn't follow his mother and instead keeps trying to open the door where the cereal is stored. Knowing Kiaan loves bacon, his mother shows him a selection of bacon pieces, crumbled sausage, and quinoa, then asks, "what would you like in your omelet?"

Kiaan predictively chooses the bacon pieces, and Mom gives him a tiny bite to taste as she puts the plate on the counter. Then, showing him tomatoes, broccoli, and sprouts asks, "which one would you like in your omelet?"

Kiaan chooses the tomatoes, and Mom again gives him a tiny portion to taste. Kiaan gives up on opening the cupboard, wanders into the living room, and begins to pace.

When the omelet is done cooking Mom calls Kiaan into the kitchen to sit at the table and eat breakfast. Kiaan ignores his mother and continues pacing. Mom tries again, and Kiaan is more direct in his protest. He begins whining and running to the other side of the room.

Placing his food on the table, Mom asks, which fruit would he like: strawberries, apples, or cantaloupe? Strawberries are his favorite fruit, and he comes over to the table to make a choice. Kiaan reaches for a strawberry while simultaneously turning to run back into the living room with it in hand. Mom pulls the bowl of strawberries back from his reach, and when he misses the grasp, he stops and looks back at where the bowl was.

Immediately, Mom asks, "Would you like to sit in your chair with a pillow under your bottom, a blanket on your lap, or all alone." Placing items briefly on the chair she reemphasizes the choices, "Pillow, blanket," and indicating an empty chair, "alone." Kiaan loves his little blue blanket and agrees to sit on the chair with his blanket in his lap. Mom arranges his food in front of him and offers him a choice of drinks. Kiaan has now settled into his old breakfast routine of eating at the table and is happy and cooperative with his mother.

Discussion

Providing structured choices to children with autism accomplishes the benefit of focused attention, a sense of personal control, and a base for pleasant interaction between caregiver and child. In the above story, Kiaan's mom has a good grasp on providing structured choices to help Kiaan feel good and remain cooperative even when his expectations are, at first, unmet. The following sections will explore the important pieces weaved throughout the story that show the benefits of providing an abundance of structured choice opportunities daily.

Benefits of Daily Structured Choice Opportunities

Focused Attention

Providing a small set of choices gives the child a positive and specific direction on which to mentally and visually focus his attention. Instead of a single request which implies a yes/no or comply/protest condition, the child now has more information to process. This focal point interrupts the child's habit to automatically protest any request in an effort to remain self-absorbed. Further, when at least one option in the set is strategically placed to entice the child, motivation to focus on the offer is enhanced. In our story Mom accomplished positive focus when tempting her son away from the cereal cupboard, encouraging him into the kitchen from the living room, and persisting in her expectation that he sits in a chair while eating his breakfast. The story reveals that Mom offered bacon as an option with the omelets to redirect Kiaan's focus from the cupboard. The strawberries were included with the fruits to move his concentration away from staying in the living room and towards communicating his preference. And, she included the offer of sitting with his favorite blanket amongst his assortment of selections to fix up his attention towards the choice and away from the expectation to sit. In other moments her select groupings were all things Kiaan liked with equal value including the vegetables and drinks allowing him a true set of choices for him to consider. Giving an abundance of small, but significant, structured choice opportunities is what keeps Kiaan's attention focused on communication and cooperation.

Empowerment

Anyone who engages with children has experienced their desire to choose the item they prefer, to play how they like, to get others to do as the child wants, or to "do it myself." These are all examples of empowerment. Many noted psychologists discuss empowerment as one of many human basic needs. All people, including small children, have a need to feel empowered. Other words that are often used when discussing this concept are power, significance, influence, and control. With empowerment, our self-confidence and self-esteem grows, helping us feel successful and worthwhile.

As we grow and learn, we practice many different behaviors to see what will satisfy our power needs. Based on the responses we receive back from others, we quickly develop consistent habits. These habits maintain the behaviors we use to help us feel our own significance.

In the beginning, parents only have a baby's crying, pushing, or pulling-away to help them learn the child's wants and interests. The baby cries, and the parents seek to satisfy the baby's needs. This is the natural healthy relationship that progresses. As children grow in social and communication skills, they try new and more creative behaviors to gain a sense of significance. These attempted behaviors become as abundant as the imagination. Behaviors may be productive and cooperative or disruptive and uncooperative. When children explore behavior strategies to gain a sense of self-empowerment, the responses of adults will shape the development of habits. Parents support the learning of new behaviors through reinforcing the actions that seem most useful within the family. Behaviors that work most often to help the children feel empowered will be displayed more regularly. The varied behaviors could be equally compliant and contrary.

Both cooperative and uncooperative means of relating to others will always be a part of every child's behavior choices. How then, do we encourage more frequent cooperative behaviors? It is a long-standing saying expressed in many proverbs that the behavior that grows and takes route is the one that is more well-fed. The way adults respond to children is the "food" that nourishes behavioral growth. Proactively engaging children also nourishes behavioral options. Structured Choice practiced abundantly is a pro-active strategy that can influence greater numbers of cooperative, engaging behaviors. By engaging the autistic child's power needs, adults can stimulate higher levels of cooperative habits. Structured Choice gives children, a sense of control within the present moment. Offering many choice opportunities throughout each day feeds the child's need to feel significant. Feeling empowered develops self-confidence. Cooperative habits grow strong and healthy, diminishing the need for protest behaviors. Structured Choice is a quick and easy way to empower children and develop cooperative habits.

When implementing Structured Choice, it is important to provide only choices that you are actually willing and able to give immediately. Limiting the choices to between two to four options helps the autistic child mentally process the offer quickly. It also helps keep the circumstance or context of the offer related to the activity at hand. Returning to Kiaan's story, you will see the context was breakfast at the table. Mom did not offer a choice of what to play with when Kiaan goes outside later. She only offered choices that mattered in the immediate present. By doing this, the child's opinion is not only asked for but also honored instantaneously. The opportunity to fulfill Kiaan's basic need for a sense of power is given freely. Kiaan's desire to protest in order to gain control is prevented. He already feels that sense of control because he made a choice. Kiaan feels well empowered!

Engagement

As is portrayed in our story, empowering children through Structured Choice does not replace the parent's responsibility to have expectations and set limits. You will recollect that Mom decided that cereal was not going to be offered and stayed firm in her decision even though Kiaan persisted in his attempts to gain access to the cereal. Mom also wanted Kiaan to eat breakfast while sitting in a chair at the table. Mom set herself up for success by making sure that Kiaan had several strongly desired choices to offer. This allowed Kiaan to focus his attention on the offered items instead of the expectations. Kiaan remained cooperative while Mom persisted in setting her limits. You will notice she did not try to bribe Kiaan by telling him if he came and followed her directions, he would get bacon and strawberries. This type of enticement eventually backfires as the child learns to understand the manipulative nature. A bribe creates a yes/no opportunity opening the door to a refusal and protest. Providing Structured Choices turns the enticement into an internal motivation for the child to communicate their desire. Structured Choice prevents getting trapped in that yes/no, win/lose argument. Offering multiple choice opportunities to children, allows them to repeatedly show their interests and likes in an appropriate and cooperative manner.

Through Structured Choice, Mom gets to know Kiaan's personal interests, which she can use in future choice opportunities. Further, Mom is given the chance to show Kiaan respect by allowing him control over some decisions throughout the day. Showing Kiaan this type of regard suggests that the child's thoughts and feelings are important to his mother. A strong, supportive, and caring relationship between the two is achieved. Is there any better feeling than thinking yourself understood, respected and loved by your parent?

Setting It Up

How Structured Choice sets are selected will depend on the particular situation. These sets are based on the availability of items or activities, and the interests and creativity of the adult. While in some cases adding an especially enticing choice may help children overcome a competing interest, the true magic is in the frequency of opportunities for children to make deliberate choices. Throughout our story, in the roughly 15 minutes it took for Mom to cook Kiaan's omelet and bring him to the table, Mom was able to offer 5 different choice opportunities. This is an average of one choice per every three minutes. That is a great start to the day! The number of choice opportunities given throughout any activity will depend on the actual activity itself. If the child is happily playing, it is not recommended that the parent interrupt play for no other purpose than to give a choice. Choices should coincide with natural instances of interaction between the adult and child. The story depicts Mom naturally speaking to Kiaan 9 times and giving him choices 5 of those times. These multiple offers of choice helped Kiaan to feel he had some control over his breakfast even if he was not permitted to eat his desired cereal.

When deciding what choices to offer it is relevant to consider the child's preferences and use a variety of interest and likability levels strategically throughout the day. The choices provided may hold a range of importance to the child including equally desirable, highly desirable, less desirable or unknown desirability options. Here are some things to consider when deciding how you will structure your choice options:

Equally Desirable Options:

- Make sure to offer a high frequency of relatively equally desired options.
- Equal options give children a true set of choices that respects and honors their personal preferences in the moment.
- Equal options may be of high, medium, or low interest.
    - Offering 3 high interest options for those times of day when the adult needs to tend to something without distraction makes sure the child is well engaged no matter the activity chosen.
    - Most options will be of medium interest. Hence is life.

- Completing chores around the house may fall in the low interest category, yet it remains an expectation of all family members. Giving a choice of which chore to complete will help in cooperation and provide the child a small sense of control within the request.

Highly Desirable Options:

- Offering a known highly desired option can provide extra motivation and interest to a child who may be holding-out hopes for some other item or activity.
- Occasionally a known highly desired option does not inspire extra motivation. Reasons for this turn-about include:
  - The items are used too often and the child no longer finds it exciting.
  - The child has grown less interested in the activity in general.
  - The child has something with a stronger motivation in mind.
  - The child is not feeling well and wants to rest.
- Not all choices can or should include highly desired items.
  - The way to move your child away from a fixation and towards other activities is to leave the fixation item out of the choice offering.
  - If only items that are known, highly preferred options are offered, the child's repertoire of skills and interests cannot be expanded.

Less Desirable Options:

- When one less desirable choice is added to three options, this helps the child to focus his attention on the higher preferred choices.

- Too many very low desired items can be detrimental to the relationship. If two of the three choices are far less desired, then you are not really offering a respectable choice. A child who regularly feels trapped into only one activity will begin to distrust the interaction and express that distrust through those protest behaviors.

- The child may surprise you from time to time and choose the usually less desirable item. Be sure you are prepared to honor that choice. Less desired options may become more preferred as the child grows and learns.

Options of Unknown Desirability:

- It is important to offer occasional options of items that either are new to the child or are of unknown preference. This will expand the child's repertoire and the parent's knowledge of the child's interests.

- Occasionally offering a set of items with only unknown interest levels within the home, will prepare your child to make choices in new environments such as community fairs. It is recommended to add an option of "No, thank you" in this case since you may not be able to predict the child's interest.

Each opportunity to offer a choice to a child is a powerful moment. The child gets to feel empowered; the parent gets to learn how the child thinks, and the engagement between the two gets to be productive and cooperative. This is a win-win-win scenario. Further, the high frequency of engagement helps the parent stay attuned to the child's physical and emotional wellbeing. Noticing any change in usually predictable responses may give parents some insight as to how the child is feeling, growing, or developing new interests. I encourage parents and caregivers to provide children as many opportunities for structured choices as can be mustered. Small choices, silly choices, creative choices, even seemingly insignificant choices. It will take you and your children a long way towards self-assurance and positive relations.

CHAPTER 3

Satiation and Fixation

Two important concepts to consider when children are struggling with engagement and cooperation include Satiation and Fixation.

Satiation

Satiation is the concept of becoming overly satisfied by something. One can become too satisfied or tired of anything. Have you ever waited for that special season to come around where your favorite treat for the year was going to be available? This treat is so special it is only made for this specific season. You are very excited with just the idea of the treat, and when you get the chance, you eat your treat with such delight. You indulge in this favorite food a little every day because it is so tempting. Then after a week or two you find that some of the treat is still sitting on the counter but you no longer find it as exciting. You do love this treat but you have frankly had enough. You have become satiated with this treat. You still like it, and next year during the same season you will repeat your enthusiasm for the indulgence. But, today you are done. You have overindulged enough this week to last you the upcoming year. You have reached Satiation.

On long weekends, and school breaks many children spend many hours a day, within their home environment. They have the same items daily with which to play. The family, unsurprisingly, engages with these items abundantly. Eventually with free access to everything, all day, day-in and day-out, it is natural that children have overindulged with their toys and activities. Also, in many homes the casual use of these items means that many of the parts of each activity has been spread around the house and are no longer easily assembled. This over-abundance of use has moved your children's interests into a state of satiation. They are bored with the toys. Further they are easily distracted away from activities when the pieces cannot be found. The children are unable to imagine another thing to do with their toys. At least, not another non-destructive or non-antagonizing thing to do with them. The mind is very creative, and finding a way to use items in ways they were not designed is always a potential. This type of interest and use may not be agreeable to parents. There are often negative consequences of such creativity. Satiation can inspire boredom, disinterest, squabbling and disruptive creativity.

Fixation

While all people are subject to the effects of satiation, families with autistic children are also contending with heightened fixation. Fixation is often expressed through self-stimulatory behavior also commonly known as stims and stimming. High frequency stereotypical and ritualistic, self-stimulatory behavior keeps kids isolated from others and inhibits social skills, and learning. This is why children with autism often have highly intensive, adult guided supports during a typical weekday. It is important to break through the fixated self-stimulatory behavior and encourage autistic children's engagement in the world around them. Many adults team up to help autistic children throughout a typical week, and parents, while the biggest part, are still only one part of that team. With the stay-at home activities during the long weekends and vacations, it is simply impossible to engage children with autism to the extent as usual. Many autistic children may begin exhibiting the opposite of satiation which is intense fixation. They have moved their engagement with toys and people in the direction of becoming more and more captivated by a limited set of interests. These children are avoiding other activities. They are also becoming more focused on their particular preoccupations. This is just as concerning a problem as satiation, if not more so. Fortunately, the strategies offered within this book will address both issues and allow parents the casual supervision needed while encouraging appropriate play and interactions with toys and family members.

In Practice

A Morning with Torin and His Family

As Mom moves around the kitchen, she is aware of her three boys shuffling around their room. The sound of the doors can be heard opening and closing several times as the boys take turns moving from the bedroom to the bathroom and back again.

"Ok, I have five more minutes before the kids come out looking for breakfast," Mom thinks to herself, "I'll just sit here and enjoy my coffee and my last few minutes of quiet." Breathing in deeply, she relishes the last moments of me time.

Five minutes later, as if set to a timer the older two boys, ages 8 and 10, launch themselves out of the room, "can we have waffles for breakfast today?"

"Sure," says Mom, "I just bought a new box. Why don't the two of you toast them up and bring the jam, butter and syrup to the table while I go help Torin get dressed".

Joining the family dressed in his vacation casual uniform of sweats and a T shirt, Dad interjects. "Butter and syrup? How about some fruit, too?"

Setting the fruit on the table, Dad offers, "We have bananas and raspberries."

As Dad and the older boys finish getting breakfast ready, Mom slips into the bedroom where she finds 5-year-old Torin deeply engrossed in stimming on his cluster of beads. Giving him a quick kiss, Mom engages, "Good morning, Torin, my love. It's almost time for breakfast, let's get you dressed."

Torin is able to dress himself, but his autism and his fixation on his beads get in the way of efficiency. Mom pulls out three pairs of pants. "Do you want blue, black, or green today?"

Torin picks the green pants, and Mom lays them on the bed with a pair of underwear. "How about a shirt; do you want dinosaur, tiger, or dog?" Torin indicates he wants the dog, and Mom lays the shirt on the bed."

Gently coaxing Torin's beads out of his hands, Mom gives him a big hug and a small tickle, then begins handing him his clothes. Noticing Torin watching her put the beads down on the floor, Mom reassures, "They are right here. Let's get dressed."

Torin completes dressing, and Mom picks up his pajamas and his beads and places them on the bed. Torin, again, watches Mom closely with some apprehension. Mom reassures for the second time, "Your beads are right here on the bed. You can play with them later today."

Then, changing the subject, Mom playfully entices, "Do you want to walk or run down the hall?" Torin smiles and begins to run ahead of his mother. As she leaves the bedroom, Mom closes the door and latches a hook to secure the door closed. She then runs up behind Torin and playfully engages him.

At the breakfast table, Dad and the older boys are already eating. Dad offers Torin his breakfast choices. Showing him two plates of waffles cut in half, Dad asks, "Do you want one waffle or two?"

Torin takes the plate with two halves. Showing him the items, Dad continues to offer, "Jam or syrup? Banana, raspberries, or both? Milk, juice, or water?" Torin makes his selections and the family finishes breakfast together.

After breakfast, Torin's brothers pull out the cars and begin to play for a while on the living room floor. Torin runs towards his bedroom and finds the door locked. He begins to fuss, and Dad approaches him. "Yes, Torin, you will play with your beads again later. Here, let's see what else you might like to do now."

Showing him some pictures of toys in the living room where his brothers are, Dad asks, "Would you like your blocks, cars, or Lincoln Logs?"

Torin picks the Lincoln Logs and plays near his brothers, who occasionally drive their cars through his structure.

After a while, Mom notices the time and comments that the older boys will have to watch their video lessons for school homework in an hour. She suggests the family go for a walk down the nearby path first. As the boys clean up, Mom stores the Lincoln Logs and their picture away on the top bookshelf to encourage Torin to pick a different toy later.

With the toys put away, the family heads out together. All three boys are walking in front of their parents down the sidewalk.

As they come around a bend, the path comes into view just beyond the large busy street. Mom asks 10-year-old Calen to hold Torin's hand. Reaching down to comply with his mother Calen attempts to take Torin's hand. Frustratingly, his brother exclaims, "Mom said! Give me your hand!"

Torin swings his arms around to avoid being held and begins to walk faster. Mom moves closer to the two, and, as the family stops at the curb Mom, catches hold of Torin. Kneeling down, she says, "Torin, we are going to cross the street, and you need your hand held. Do you want to hold hands with Mommy, Daddy, or Brother?

Dad makes an excited face and extends his hand, enticing Torin, 'I'll walk with you!"

Taking his father's hand, Torin agrees to walk with Dad, and the family safely crosses the street together.

After returning from the walk, Mom instructs the older boys to get their things ready at the dining room table for their video time. Dad sets off to prepare the computer for the lesson.

Torin again runs to his bedroom and finds it locked. Mom engages him, "Yes Torin, you can play with you beads in a little while." Showing him two pictures, she instructs, "first puzzles, then beads," and hands him the puzzle picture. Torin accepts the picture and goes to the living room which opens to the dining room where his brothers are.

Sitting at the coffee table Torin is given options of which puzzles to complete. With Mom's help, Torin does well playing with the puzzles.

After about 25 minutes, Torin begins standing up from his little chair, making increasing amounts of noise and twiddling the puzzle pieces through his fingers. Mom recognizes this behavior as a cue of his fatigue with this activity and the potential for Torin to begin fussing very soon. Knowing that Torin's brothers still need another 30 minutes of quiet time for the video lesson she offers Torin his beads and asks. "Where would you like to play? On the couch, in the big chair, or over in the corner, Mom indicates a different area of the living room further from the dining room. Torin picks the big chair and Mom lets him enjoy his beads.

When the older boys are done with their video lesson, Dad suggests they go play outside for a while before taking on the next lesson. Mom engages Torin saying, "OK, sweetie, time to go outside."

Torin stims a bit more frantically for a moment, and then Mom again cajoles the beads away from him and offers him a choice of outside activities to play. Torin chooses to ride his bicycle and joins his brothers in the yard. Mom puts the beads back on the bed and locks the bedroom door.

Discussion

So, how do we overcome satiation and fixation without buying a houseful of new toys? Choice and structure will go a long way in helping with these issues while getting through long days at home. Further, as in many other things, moderation is crucial. Throughout a typical weekday, moderation of household toys and activities is inbuilt. School children are not at home for many hours on weekdays, and have other activities that compete with their opportunity to play at home.

During holidays and vacations, to overcome satiation and fixation parents will need to manufacture this moderation. The focal point is organizing and limiting access to toys and activities in order to keep play interesting and varied. This is not in the spirit of punishing, but of reigniting and reinforcing a variety of interests.

As you will notice in the story above, Torin's parents keep his bedroom door locked after he gets dressed in the morning. By doing so they are able to prevent Torin from accessing his stimming beads at every opportunity. When Torin tries to get his beads, his parents acknowledge his interest, and address his desire. They do not reprimand him for trying to get his beads or tell him, "No, you can't play with them." Mom and Dad simply indicate a sentiment of "Yes, but later." Immediately after this communication, they offer Torin a choice of activities to do. Responding to Torin in this manner keeps him focused on what is next instead of protesting what is lost.

Later in the story. you notice Mom putting the Lincoln Logs on the top bookshelf. She will not offer these to Torin again until tomorrow. Instead she will encourage him to play with the other toys in that area on his next opportunity. This strategy both moderates the access to the Lincoln Logs to maintain their interest and requires Torin to play with a larger variety of toys expanding his range of activities.

Are you ready to fight back against satiation and fixation brought about by long hours and multiple days at home? The following chapters will examine ways to clean up, organize, set limits and engage children through Structured Choice. I realize this may feel like a lot of work. And, You may imagine it will spark more arguments as the children will not want to have their free access to toys limited. But, I assure you, it will reignite interest and reduce the agitation that comes with boredom, satiation, and intense fixation. This may be a big job in the beginning but it is a one-time clean-up followed by easy to manage follow through. It is totally worth the effort. The following chapters will walk you through steps for structuring up your environment, toys, and daily schedule, while infusing Structured Choice opportunities throughout. I again promise I am not going to be advocating a strict educational approach to managing your autistic children at home. I offer just a few tricks to keep their interest in a variety of activities and reduce those difficult moments of agitation.

CHAPTER 4

Environmental Structure

Identifying purpose, organizing ideas, and planning are at the heart of any change process. In this chapter I give some simple ideas with examples that will help you prepare mentally and, if desired, environmentally for including choice and structure in your home routines. Dedicating the time to organize your home environment will be an effort worth the undertaking. The following suggestions may take as little or as much time and energy as you choose. Some suggestions may require you a hearty surge of exertion to get you started and others may simply require you to make a mental note of the information. Nonetheless, you are the one who chooses what information speaks to your needs. Let's look at the steps that will move you towards the goal of developing choice and structure practices.

Preparing the Toys

Step One

The first step in this process, as in all processes, is to clean-up and get organized. First pull all the toy parts together. Are the puzzle pieces spread out around the house? Have the farm animals made it into the bathroom, under the couch, on top the TV and in the beds? What about the blocks, cars, game pieces and fancy parts to the doll house? Have their boxes and decorative containers become empty? Well then, it's time for a round-up. Get all those toys back together with their original groups. Once this is done the kids may want to start playing with the toys again because they can see the purpose of the items, all the parts are obvious. Congratulations! You have begun to see the benefits already! Don't stop there. I offer you even more success.

Step Two

Now that you can see what you have, divide the toys into like items by either function of play, or area of play. This can be a simple mental activity or you can actually physically organize the toys into these categories.

- Function of play examples:
    - Art and craft related
    - Writing and education, science related items
    - Imagination play with props such as farm, doll house, army
    - Musical instruments and rhythm toys
    - Watch and listen to items such as TV, videos, tablet, and radio
    - Building and assembling items such as blocks, Lincoln logs, magnet and construction sets
    - Manipulative items such as marble mazes and cars on tracks

- Problem solving such as puzzles, tangrams, and models
- Board and card games
- Inside movement - dance and fitness items
- Outside movement - bikes, balls, etc

- Area of play examples:

  - Stay in one spot or couch, comfy chair, and bed items such as books, musical toys, & electronic games
  - Sitting at a table such as table games, writing, table puzzles, art, crafts, and cooking activities
  - Spread out around the floor such as building items, blocks, floor puzzles, Doll house, and farm set
  - Indoor clear floor space for inside appropriate motor activities such as fitness, dance, or pacing needs
  - Outdoor play spaces for both high energy activities, and quieter activities

Identifying Zones of Play

After organizing the toys, let's consider your general environment. Take a look around and see how many different kid friendly spaces you can identify. Yes, most of your house is a kid friendly space, but I want you to think in more definitive pockets of space, or zones of play. This may be simple for those who live in a house with a yard. But even if you live in a one room studio or hotel, you can discover several explicitly identifiable areas. Try to be as specific as possible in your own home. Here are some examples:

House with yard:

- Living room
    - on the couch
    - on the floor
    - at the coffee table.

- Bedroom
    - On the bed
    - On the floor

- Kitchen/Dining room
    - Sitting at the table
    - At the sink/ counter

- Bathroom
    - In the tub/shower
    - At the sink/mirror

- Outside
    - On the patio
    - On the driveway/walkway
    - In the grass

Studio apartment/hotel

- On the bed
- On the floor to the right side of the bed
- On the floor to the left side of the bed

- On the floor at the foot of the bed
- In a chair
- In front of the TV
- Sitting at the table
- In a hallway
- In the bath tub/shower
- At the sink/mirror
- Outside in a public space/side walk/trail/green belt

In Practice

A Day with Francesca

Awakening to another morning, 10-year-old Francesca searches her bed for her favorite doll. She finds it stuffed between the bed and the wall and pulls it out with a strong tug. Francisca's doll has long brown hair and a long skinny body. This doll fits perfectly in Francisca's hand allowing Francesca to wrap all her fingers around the body and keep a firm grasp on the doll. Once she has the doll in hand, Francesca lays on the floor and shakes the doll over her face allowing the light from window to filter through the shiny brown strands of hair as they bounce about. After a while, Dad enters Francisca's room and greets her with a warm, "good morning, beautiful."

Francesca sings with glee as the doll's hair shakes and bounces in the light. Dad moves around the room, picking up and making the bed before he engages Francesca again, "Ok, honey, it's time for breakfast."

Helping her to her feet, Dad gives Francesca a hug, then instructs, "Ok, where is dolly going to wait for you? On the bed, the dresser, or the chair?" Francesca avoids her dad and shakes dolly in the air a few more times. Dad repeats his question, and Francesca finally throws dolly onto the bed. Francesca runs to the kitchen.

Following behind her, Dad asks, "Which cereal are you going to pick today?" He opens the cupboard door where the top shelf has several boxes of cereal displayed. Francesca grabs her oat clusters and bounces over to the table with the box.

After eating, Francesca wanders to the back door and looks out onto the yard. Dad says, "If you want to go outside, you need to get dressed. "

Francesca stands at the door, singing to herself. Dad approaches her with two pictures, "Do you want to get dressed, or stay in your pajamas?" Francesca picks pajamas, and Dad leaves her to look out the door for a while longer.

Eventually, Francesca begins to bounce around the house, and Dad says, "Oh, I can see you are ready for another activity." Showing her three pictures, he asks do you want to color, play blocks, or dance?

Francesca picks dancing, and Dad says, "Ok, you have to dance on the dance floor."

Dad shows her a picture identifying the empty space in the living room between the couch and the TV. Francesca runs to the space and jumps around excitedly. Dad gives her choices of music, and Francesca dances around the room for 45 minutes.

When Francesca tires she runs to her room, grabs her dolly, and lies on the bed, shaking the doll's hair. Dad follows her, saying, "Well, as long as you are in your bedroom, let's get you dressed."

Francesca shakes her doll above her head while Dad prepares her clothes. After being given a choice of outfits, Francesca gets dressed while keeping a firm grasp on her doll.

Once Francesca is completely dressed, Dad offers her three choices of activities outside. She picks to play with sidewalk chalk and tries to run out of the room with her doll in hand. Dad reminds her to put the doll down by offering her choices of where to have dolly wait. Disappointed, Francesca throws her doll back on the bed and goes outside to the driveway.

There is a box of outside toys near the driveway. Dad opens the box and gets out the chalk.

After drawing some pictures for a while, Francesca starts jumping around and throwing the chalk up in the air and catching it. Dad suggests she go play in the grass for a while and has her choose from three higher energy grass appropriate toys. Francesca and Dad kick the soccer ball around the yard for about 30 minutes before heading to the patio to cool down.

Lunch time approaches, and the two go inside to eat at the table. Choices are offered, and the meal is enjoyed. Before leaving the table, Dad offers Francesca a choice of the living room or the back yard again. He knows she would rather stim with her doll right now, but he has a conference call to make in an hour and wants her busy during that time.

Francesca chooses the living room and puzzles. She goes to the toy chest in the corner of the living room and dad helps her pull out several puzzles. Later, Dad decides Francesca needs to burn some energy and sends her outside offering her skates, bikes, and swing. Francesca chooses to skate and obtains her skating equipment from the outdoor toy box.

Before making the conference call, the two return indoors. Dad gives Francesca some choices of her tablet, her doll, or watching cartoons on the couch. Francesca predictively chooses her doll and enjoys her time stimming while Dad focuses on his video meeting from his home office.

Later in the afternoon, the two go for a walk in the neighborhood and then watch cartoons in the living room. Dad offers Francesca some art activities, and she goes to the cabinet in the dining room to pick from supplies. Francesca decides to paint in the dining room.

Later, Francesca and Dad go back outdoors and Francesca chooses to ride her bike. Dad shows her a picture of her bike helmet, and she obtains it from the outside box. The two take a bike ride around the block. Francesca has been happy today. All the structured choices, visual cues, and environmental organization dad used kept her agreeable and engaged.

Discussion

You have collected toys and sorted them by function or area of play. Multiple kid-friendly spaces or zones of play have been identified in your home. Let's blend these two topics. Think about where in your home your children typically play. Do you have a preference where you would like the kids to play with certain toys? Perhaps, currently your children take all toys anywhere around the house, but maybe you would prefer those science experiments and soccer balls stay outside.

Possibly you wish the markers were used at a table so the couch doesn't get colored. How about the electronic toys? I'll bet you instruct that they not be played in the bath tub. And do you really want all those blocks scattered about the kitchen floor, or the farm animals populating the hallway?

It's time to decide where each kind of toy would be best played. If you like, you can even store sets of like toys accordingly around the home to coincide with those locations. If keeping them in one place, or where you have always kept them works best for you, then do that. You will notice that throughout Francesca's day in the tale above, she was finding toys in the location that dad suggested she should play. The sidewalk chalk, soccer ball, skating and bike equipment were in the outside toy box. Her puzzles were in the inside toy box. Art supplies were located near the dining room for quick access. This made it easy to monitor Francesca's transitions without having to find toys scattered around the house. How you store toys is completely up to you. This is your home. The important point is to encourage specific areas of play and consider how easy or difficult it will be to support these activities in real life.

As the day progressed, Dad was able to easily take advantage of his structure, zones of play, and pre-planning of time and energy to maximize both Francesca's needs and his own. Looking back at Francesca's story, you will notice that Dad strategically moved her around the home when offering activities. Changing areas with each activity helped to alert her sensory system and offer her a new place to focus her attention. This focus and the many transitions throughout the day kept her engaged in a variety of toys. Dad's pre-planning of play zones resulted in each area having specific attributes which delivered predictable boundaries resulting in successful and safe play. In the living room, she danced in an open space between the couch and TV. She also played with puzzles in a corner out of the way of walking spaces, and sat on the couch for more sedentary activities. In the dining room she ate her meals and engaged in art activities. Outside, the play areas naturally occurred for each activity including chalk and skates on the drive way, soccer in the grass and bikes in the neighborhood. By organizing her toys into similar functions and areas of play he kept transitions quick and simple. Utilizing clear zones of play, Dad helped Francesca understand, and accept boundaries.

Now, if this is feeling a bit too structured for a home, remember that children with autism thrive on structure! The predictability and routine help them to understand expectations and regulate their own anxiety, over stimulation, and fatigue. Give it a try; see if you like it.

CHAPTER 5

The Dance

Leading with structured choice, planning, and arranging the dance between space, energy, and time will stimulate even greater levels of success. Play all day can be quite enjoyable for children with autism when assistance and structured choices are provided. By strategically using spaces around the home, changing-up the energy level throughout the day, and identifying timing that supports the child's attention span, parents can help their child interact positively. This may sound a little daunting but many of these things are already naturally occurring in your home. Merely taking notice, and making some small tweaks may be all that is needed.

Structured Choices

The act of simply offering a choice will engage the interest of a child enough to be able to focus on activities. Choice can be offered for location, toys, actions, activities, materials, daily living routines such as dressing, bathing, chores, and of course food and drink. When offering choices parents maintain as much or as little control over the options as they please.

Parents can choose the location and the activity, then offer the child a choice of materials.

An example would be to tell your child, "We will sit at the table and color. Would you like to color with markers or crayons?"

After the first choice is made, a second is given, "Which picture would you like to color?"

Alternately, parents could choose the location and offer the choice of both activity and materials. An example would be telling a child, "We are going to sit at the table. Would you like to color or do puzzles?"

Then, once coloring is chosen, the question might be, "Are you going to color with markers, crayons, or pencils?"

If appropriate, parents could also offer choices of location, activity, and materials. For instance, "Where would you like to play next?"

Once at the location (table), parents could offer, "Do you want puzzles, coloring, or writing?"

After the child picks coloring, the offer could be made, "Are you going to color with markers, crayons, or pencils?"

All choices are adult-driven and child-centered. I have even ventured to offer silly choices that speak to mood and energy like, "Shall we color while singing, making silly noises, or listening to music?"

Space

Effectively utilizing the space around the home will support children's active engagement in activities. The simple act of moving locations around the home activates the physical and sensory systems to help children to become more alert and interested in the surrounding environment. Moving from one room or area in a room to another brings about a mental attentiveness. This mental state helps the children engage their interest in the materials within the new location.

It is good to move around the home as often as your children need, but make sure to stay in different locations for some period of time so there isn't just an hour of wandering. Some concepts to keep in mind when considering the use of space include:

- Try to move to at least three different locations around the home before repeating a previous location.

- When returning to a space in the home try to offer different play activities with similar space needs. For instance, if in the morning we sat at the table and colored in coloring books with markers, then in the afternoon we will sit at the table and write with colored pencils on blank paper. Same location, similar activities but different materials.

- When changing locations be sure to accommodate fluctuating energy needs. Energy is discussed later in this chapter.

- It is beneficial to make a mental note of the daily schedule for the entire family so that you may plan ahead and account for your needs and the needs of siblings when offering activities. For example, if you know your older child will be needing help with school work at the table at 10:00 AM then plan for that. Does your child with autism need to be at the table with you? Then make sure the activities within the previous hour are done somewhere else and engage higher energy levels. Or, if your autistic child needs to be away from the table and otherwise engaged, make sure to schedule the activities to best support those needs.

- It is helpful to identify spaces that serve different functions and energy levels.

    o Stay in one spot and relax - couch, comfy chair, and bed
    o Sitting at a table can be kitchen table, coffee table, or kids table
    o Open floor space that is not in the way of high traffic areas. This space may be used for activities where materials get spread across the floor
    o Indoor clear space needs for motor activities such as fitness or dance and sing
    o Outdoor areas for high movement activities such as balls bikes, running, tumbling
    o Outdoor areas for low movement activities sidewalk chalk, science experiments, messy sensory play

Energy

Being aware of the energy levels inherent for different types of activities will help you to offer choices that will keep your child well-regulated throughout the day. Below are just a few examples:

- Low energy activities: things done on couches, comfy chairs and beds that take mostly mental and visual effort, or no effort- reading, writing, coloring, TV, video games, Tablet, sensory activities, and resting or naps.

- Medium energy activities: manipulative play items - Things done at a table or on the floor that takes mental and low physical effort- Blocks, cars, puzzles, farm and doll houses, sidewalk chalk, dolls, marble maze, cars on tracks, spinning toys.

- High Energy; things done that requires greater physical effort - Dancing, tickles, wrestling, crawling around, tumbling, bouncing, balls, climbing, walking, running jumping, chasing, bikes, skates etc...

When considering energy, it is also important to identify your child's subtle cues as to when a change of energy is needed. About how long can your child last in different activities before becoming distracted, bored, hyper, whinny or destructive? When noticed early you can prevent behaviors that might become inappropriate and lead to reprimands, and tantrums. Some questions to consider are:

- Does your daughter get squirmy when sitting too long? Or, does it depend on what she is doing while sitting. I know many children who can only sit for 5-10 minutes with a book, but if allowed, would not move from their spot for hours while playing video games. Both of these things are good to know when deciding what to offer as a choice for the next activity.

- How long can your son play before engaging with his toy in a way for which it was not designed? Time to Change-it up! This definitely leads to disruptive activities, reprimands, and punishments! Keep things light and suggest a switch.

- Does your little girl start to focus more on stim items when she is getting physically, or mentally tired? Take notice and move to a relaxing activity or even offer a limited amount of time for self-stimulation to meet her needs.

- Can your darling boy handle medium energy activities without quickly escalating his physical movement? Or, should he engage in high energy activities first, so he is sufficiently tired enough to play appropriately with the blocks without throwing them around the room?

- Many children progress regularly from medium level to high level energy as they become bored with the first activity. If you see an increase in physical movement, this might be a good time to suggest a new more physically engaging play choice in another location. When a toy car driving activity becomes demolition derby then maybe it is time to suggest riding bikes or playing basketball.

- Is there going to be a busy parent time? Will you need the child to remain in one place for easy supervision while cooking, cleaning, fixing something, or engaging with siblings? It would be best if an extremely high energy activity happens before this quite/still time. Tucker those kiddos out. Then give them a highly desirable, quiet time activity such as those fixation items, movie or video game activities.

- Most of the time you will automatically know the energy level your child needs, but sometimes you just can't tell. A child might become fussy because he has not moved enough and needs to get up and run around. Or, the child might be fussy because he is coming down with a cold and really just needs a lot of low and medium energy activities. When you don't know, it is a great time to start your choice offer with questioning where they might like to go for the next activity - the couch, play room, or outside. The child will be happy to let you know what they need. Once in the location you can give a choice of what activity they want to do.

Time

Different activities have different time tolerance levels or take different amounts of time to accomplish. Usually 30 minutes is an average tolerance for many children with autism, except when engaged in highly preferred or very low preferred activities. When planning for how long you think an activity might last, consider:

- The child's tolerance levels for the activity, for example:
    - Reading - 5 minutes
    - Video game - 1 hour
    - Blocks - 20 minutes
    - Chase and tickle - 20 minutes

- Coloring - 30 minutes
- Changing over the laundry - 5 minutes
- Eating breakfast - 20 minutes
- Stim on wheels and pace - 1 hour

- How long does it take the child to complete an activity like a puzzle or coloring page?
- Will it matter to the child if the activity is stopped before the task is finished? If it takes the child 15 minutes to complete a puzzle then don't offer him a puzzle 10 minutes before you need to move him to another location so a sibling can use the table for a school assignment. Plan ahead for the timing needed.
- Are there other activities that need to be managed or planned for at the same time? Do siblings have competing needs for the location or materials, do you have competing needs for the location or materials?

In Practice

An Afternoon with Alissa

Enjoying her lunch, 15-year-old Alissa carefully keeps her grapes, carrots, and sandwich separated on her plate. She eats very deliberately finishing her carrots first, then her sandwich and lastly slowly savors each grape. Her 2-younger sisters are sitting at the dining table with her. They are eating and discussing music they like. As lunch comes to an end, the little girls ask Mom if they can play the dance-along video on the television. Mom considers their request. Thinking that the children's father will be home in an hour from working a long shift at the hospital and that Alissa also likes this activity, Mom agrees to the girl's request.

Alissa's sisters get things set up, and, handing her a dancing picture, ask if Alissa wants to play. Alissa happily cleans up her lunch items and goes to the indicated open space in the living room. The younger girls have picked the first song and they all dance together. When the music stops mom insists that the girls give Alissa a turn to choose and the girls offer Alissa three pictures of songs they know she likes. The girls play and dance for a full hour taking turns choosing music videos. When Dad arrives home they excitedly show him some dance moves.

Soon, Mom tells the girls it is time to quiet down so Dad can take a nap. Mom closes the TV cabinet and delivers instructions to the girls. Alissa's sisters are asked to go to their rooms and complete their reading assignments for school. Mom offers Alissa a set of quieter activities to do in her room as well.

After 15 minutes of quiet, Alissa begins pacing in her room. Realizing Alissa is bored and will begin to be louder soon, Mom offers Alissa to come into the kitchen and help put away the lunch dishes. The dishes activity only lasts 10 minutes so Mom sends Alissa to the dining room to pick a calming coloring activity to do. Alissa picks her favorite art book and a set of pastel markers from the nearby cabinet. She sits in the dining room while coloring, but this interest only lasts about 15 minutes. Alissa is then instructed to return to the living room space between the couch and TV but this time she is requested to do some yoga moves with mom. Allowing Alisa to choose the positions helps her to engage cooperatively with Mom for another 20 minutes.

After a successfully quiet hour mom encourages all three girls to go outside and enjoy hot the afternoon sun. Alissa's sisters are riding their bikes and Alissa jumps on the trampoline.

After Dad has awoken from his nap, he joins the girls outside and encourages all three to come into the shade on the patio and play with some silly putty he made. Alissa doesn't want to get off the trampoline, but when Dad gives her a choice of sitting at the table in a chair, on a large ball, or standing, she willingly chooses to sit on the large ball.

After some time enjoying the coolness, slimy feeling, and jiggly texture of the silly putty the girls start throwing it on each other. Alissa joins in the fun but throws the putty too hard. Dad realizes this activity is getting out of hand and suggests cleaning up. The girls are not pleased with Dad's suggestion but when he offers Alissa the choice to wash-up in the bathroom or the hose, they realize they get to play in the water and agreeably clean up.

After a fun afternoon in the sun, Mom brings the group some towels and requests they come inside and get changed. Mom helps Alissa change, brings her into the living room, and offers her the choice to sit on the couch, chair, or bean bag chair while watching cartoons. Alissa picks the bean bag chair and settles in for TV time with her sisters while Mom and Dad talk and prepare dinner. It has been a fun afternoon for Alissa and her sisters.

Discussion

Considering the space, energy, and time needs of your family will help in planning activities over the course of a few hours. When deciding on a progression of activities, keeping some of the ideas presented in this chapter in mind will be useful. Some applicable details include:

- Avoid repeating the same activity with the same materials, in the same space on the same day.
- Try to move spaces without repeating the same space for three rotations.
- Acknowledge your children's changing energy levels and plan activities with them in mind.
- Awareness of time factors of each activity will aide effective planning.

Remember, we are trying to create a system of moderation to keep the kids interested and engaged with a variety of toys. To effectively realize this aim, we must moderate their use. Now, this is not to say that your child can't repeat the general activity at different times of the day, or use the same spaces for similar activities. Just mix it up somehow. For instance, if in the morning your daughter colors at the dining table, with markers, in the princess coloring book, then maybe in the evening she could color at the coffee table with colored pencils in the baby animal coloring book.

Looking at Alissa's story you will see that Mom managed space by moving the girls around the home effectively. The family moved fluidly from the dining room to the living room then the bed rooms. When Alissa needed to change-things-up after quiet time in her bedroom, mom brought her into the kitchen then the dining table before returning to the living room. The simple act of changing environments helped Alissa remain engaged and cooperative with the expectation to remain relatively quiet.

Mom honored Alissa's movement and energy needs over the afternoon by planning ahead and being creative. Knowing there would be an hour of expected quiet, mom agreed to Alissa and her sisters dancing to burn off energy. Later Alissa needed another movement activity so mom helped her do yoga. These activities used the same space and engaged physical activity but were different actions and energy levels. These thoughtful changes kept things interesting for Alissa and maintained cooperation.

Mom also strategically managed time needs for Alissa. Mom knew that dancing is a favorite activity of all three girls and would last a long time. Thinking that this will help them be quiet while dad is napping, Mom gladly agreed to the dancing.

As the story progresses we see that Alissa needed to change her quiet activities repeatedly in the hour that her father napped because her tolerance level for each activity was only 10-20 minutes. Mom continued to expect quiet activities while also honoring Alissa's attention span. Mom's allowance of changes in activities based on Alissa's timing needs, maintained Alissa's compliance with expectations and her interest in activities.

Integrating Structured Choice Options When Planning the Day

Here are some more tips to consider when planning your day and integrating the Structured Choice options.

- Plan high energy activity choices before a time when the parent would prefer the child be engaged in more quiet and still activities.

- Plan highly desired independent activities for busy parent times.

- Include fixation items a couple times a day. Often, these do serve a purpose to regulate children with autism's systems/anxieties. But make a point to give specific time frames and stay consistent. Stim activities may also work well as a highly preferred activity for busy parent times.

- Not just play: Chores and daily living skills such as cleaning up, eating, bathing and dressing are easily included in the system of Choice and Structure. This could really become a lifestyle habit if you desire. The following is an example of offering choice during a chore task.

    o Offer a choice of which chore to complete asking, "would you like to dust, sweep, or pick up clothes?"
    o Offer a tool to use within that chore. For instance, if your daughter chooses to dust ask, "do you choose the blue, green or orange dusting rag?"

- o Offer a silly choice for emotion support and motivation such as, "while dusting, do you want to dance silly, sing loudly, or clean quietly?"

- Check in on your own needs. Do you have the energy to supervise bikes, skates, and soccer outside, or would it be easier to let the kids bounce on the mini trampoline or dance and sing inside for a while? Don't offer an activity that you are unprepared or unwilling to supervise. Do you need to use the restroom or just sit down with a favorite drink for a few minutes? Then offer your children activities that allow for minimal supervision and parental interaction. Knowing your own need status, and offering you children choices that support this status is a gift to the entire family. You are a major part of the relationship, mood, and energy dynamics. You are far better at engaging the children with structured choice, cooperative play, and patient supervision when your own needs are adequately met.

CHAPTER 6

Comprehension and Communication

There are several ways in which parents can increase comprehension and communication with their children with autism. These include cues, visual supports, and scheduling.

Cues

Children with autism need clear and predictable cues to help them know what to do, when to do things, where to go, or what to get. Basically, they need cues to assist their comprehension of your requests. You may or may not be aware of it, but you are already using predictable cues with your children to let them know what expectations you have. A cue is anything that is done, said, shown, or positioned to signal an to act, refrain from acting, or indicate that there will be upcoming information. A cue can be as obvious as standing in front of your child with a ball and asking, "Do you want to play basketball?" A cue can also be as subtle as raising an eyebrow and taking a deep breath before answering a request for another chocolate bar. With this breath, most children already know the answer is, "NO."

Children with autism, by nature of the diagnosis, do not pick up on subtle cues. They will stand waiting in anticipation for your answer until it is clearly and determinately given. The answer is spoken, "NO," and the candy is put on the top shelf of the cupboard. Using clear, obvious cues that supports the child's developmental, social, and communication skills is extremely important for children with autism.

Cues may be delivered through a variety of senses including auditory, physical/tactile, visual, and environmental means.

- An auditory cue is anything that can be heard. It includes simple sounds such as the beep of the microwave, ringing of the phone, or the sound of the timer alarm. Spoken words are also auditory cues. In the common language of autism practitioners, talking is referred to as verbal cues or verbal prompts. Auditory cues are considered fleeting pieces of information because as soon as the sound ends the information is no longer available. Children with autism do well with simple auditory cues like a timer to help them know when it is time to clean up. Verbal cues which hold more complex information are far more difficult for children with autism to process. Verbal cues need to be used very deliberately with limited specific wording.

- Physical/tactile cues are those that engage touch. A tap on the arm to gain a child's attention or slight press on their back to help them know when it is time to walk forward are simple physical cues. Physical cues are good supports for autistic children when teaching new skills. Gently tapping a child on the arm to remind him to complete an action is a typical physical cue. Physical cues can also be disruptive in some situations. A good example is when you are trying to leave the park and you place your hand on your child's back to let him know to begin walking to the car. If your child wants to protest leaving, this touch may ignite a tantrum.

- Environmental cues include, space, walls and objects around the area. A closed door indicates that the bathroom is not currently accessible. Mom placing a pillow on the floor in front of the TV indicates a comfy place to sit while watching cartoons. Environmental cues are very strong supports for children with autism.

- Visual cues are anything that can be seen. Many visual cues used with autistic children include the real objects, real pictures, line drawings, gestures, pantomime and written words. With the abundant use of electronic devices such as smart phones and tablets many families are using pictures on these devices to aide in providing visual cues. For instance, if you are asking your son to get in the car you could have a picture of the car or the car-seat on your phone to show as a visual cue to help him understand the request. Printed visual cues including electronic pictures, are the most successfully used cues for children with autism. A printed visual cue is static and continuous. The information remains available to process for as long as the child can look at it. Unlike auditory cues or fleeting visual cues such as gestures and pantomime, a printed visual cue can be continuously re-referenced to aide in remembering the information across time and location. Pictured visual cues can be used in the absence of objects, and are far easier to travel with than objects. Pictured visual cues, especially electronic versions are our autism super stars! I strongly suggest the use of pictured visual cues to support children with autism.

Visual Supports

Visual supports are the most important receptive and expressive communication aides for a child with autism. A visual support is anything that can be seen that helps children with autism understand and communicate. Visual supports include both the visual cues and the environmental cues discussed above. A child can see a closed door and pillow as well as gestures, objects, pictures and words. Autistic children are known to process information better through vision than through hearing. They are visual learners. They are also visual communicators.

Visual supports can be of a fleeting nature. They can also be static in nature.

Fleeting Visual Supports

Fleeting visual supports include gestures and pantomime. If Dad waves to his son to come towards him then puts his hand down, the wave gesture disappears. It is no longer available information for the son to see. Similarly, if Mom indicates her daughter should wash her hands before eating lunch by rubbing them together, that information disappears when mom stops. It is only accessible to the girl while Mom is acting out the movements.

Static Visual Supports

Static visual supports are those things that remain available to be seen across time. Objects, pictures and positions of furniture in the room remain available for referencing long after the initial presentation. This static nature is very helpful to children with autism. The permanent nature allows autistic children time to process information. Static visual supports also allow the flexibility to return attention to the information again and again for as long as it is in sight.

Visual supports are essential to the positive engagement of children with autism. For most children, printed visual supports raise the strength of assistance greatly. For the benefit of this discussion, I include any electronic illustration such as pictures and words on smart phones and tablets as a printed visual support. The power of printed visual supports lies in their stay-ability across time and their portability across environments. It is far easier to indicate to your daughter that she is to sit in the swing by showing her a picture of the swing and by taking it with her as she exits the house. After she breaches the threshold of the door onto the patio she may see a ball and begin to run towards it. At this time, you can remind her she is meant to go to the swing by reengaging her visual attention towards the picture. Printed Visual supports travel easily. Electronic devices travel well and can quickly be used to add new pictures on a moment's notice. The ability to quickly add a picture to your collection is extremely helpful.

Pictured Visual Supports are magic aides for children with autism and intellectual challenges. I encourage parents to become familiar with using them in as many interactions as possible. Visual supports that are used as cues helps children receive information and tell the children what is expected of them. This is known as receptive communication. The same materials are available for children to express their wants and needs to their families. This is known as expressive communication. Children with autism who struggle with spoken communication, can use static visual supports to express their wants and needs. Many children can learn how to utilize these supports to independently approach others and make requests. In this book I have focused on using them when helping children through the offer of choices. No matter the reason all forms of visual supports are indispensably beneficial for children with autism.

Visual Schedules

Visual schedules are organized lists indicating the order of activities. These schedules can be simple whole day plans or multi layered to include the different steps of individual activities. The schedules themselves can be presented as sets of individual pictures that are pulled off one at a time as each activity is completed, or simple written lists to reference the daily plan.

Visual schedules are strongly fortified and readily used in schools and in-home therapy support programs. With good intentions, parents and caregivers may be enthusiastically encouraged to use detailed picture schedules at home. Weather these schedules get used or not varies from not at all, to only during in-home therapy, to systematically throughout the day

- most days. I would venture though that most families are of the not-at-all to rarely group. Reasons for the chosen use of visual schedules in the home are as varied as the individual families involved.

Below are some common reasons families choose not to use visual schedules.

1. The home environment is far more easy-going, low structured and free flowing than school and therapy settings.
2. Children with Autism are comfortable with home routines and do not need constant reference to a schedule to move between activities in the home.
3. Repeatedly directing a child to a schedule can be more work than necessary.
4. Referencing children to the schedule in every activity can be more cumbersome and stressful for parent and child.
5. Parents have multiple things to manage within the home at any moment, whereas schools and therapists are structured specifically to guide and teach the child with autism. Visual schedule use is part of the plan.
6. Materials to maintain the schedules often get misplaced, lost, broken etc. This makes it difficult for families to maintain consistent practice.
7. Children's ability to more fluidly choose activities throughout the day is inhibited by inflexible, pre-programed schedules.
8. Families feel that it is not a necessary practice. Schedules feel too rigid and cumbersome.

I maintain that these are all valid and appropriate points! Home life is simply not school or therapy!

And…

Understanding the big picture of visual schedules and finding a way to routinely make them available in the home is helpful.

Within the daily, routine, predictable, happenings of home life, there is no need for a visual schedule. Children with autism learn and rely heavily on routines and internalize them easily. No one will feel the least bit stressed within these parameters.

The trouble comes when there is a change. Any change. On a Saturday lacking plans, eating breakfast before getting dressed, because- well it's a lazy Saturday morning, can trigger a meltdown. Why? Well, the child's understanding of the routines of the house are now shattered. The day is no longer predictable. Anxiety quickly engulfs your precious off spring. Parents lament, "Why can't the family just lay around and watch TV all morning while munching on breakfast foods without chaos?" Simply because of confusion and lack of communication. Schedules are *communication*.

If children learn to use visual schedules, their internal predictions of the events can be re-written by simply helping them understand that today's order of events is going to be different. Reducing anxiety during change is the biggest benefit of schedules. Communicating what is *different* will benefit the entire family!

Cues, visual supports and schedules are important, but as shown in the following story they do not need to be overwhelming, or difficult. As previously stated, Home is not School or Therapy! A strict adherence to using these strategies for every little thing is not advocated. Simply making them available and becoming comfortable communicating through these means, provides the needed supports.

In Practice

An Evening with Jinho

"Time to eat, Jinho," Mom calls out from the kitchen. Jinho is deeply engrossed in his game on his tablet and does not respond to his mother. "Jinho," she calls out again. Still no response. Bringing a plate with her, Mom approaches Jinho. Running her hand down the length of his arm, she gently breaks his trance. As he looks her way, Mom holds up the plate repeating, "Time to eat."

Hungry from a long day of playing and the smell of dinner cooking, Jinho quickly puts down his tablet and heads towards the dining table. Placing her hand on his shoulder, Mom stops Jinho. When he turns to see why she stopped him, Mom pantomimes hand washing and requests "Wash your hands, please." Jinho knows this predictable routine well and willingly complies.

Returning to the table with his family, Jinho sits and happily awaits his food. The family pauses to give thanks for their meal before eating. Jinho begins gesturing towards the bowl in front of him, and his dad taps his hand lightly, then makes an overexaggerated motion of placing his own hands together in a position of prayer. Jinho imitates his father and waits patiently for his sister to complete her recital. The family then enjoys a delightful meal.

As the meal ends and the family clears their plates from the table, Mom takes a moment to alert Jinho to his schedule hanging on the wall. As this is a mostly free-choice day, Jinho's schedule only has pictures of, get dressed, play, meals, restroom, shower, and bed. Mom crosses off the previous play time and dinner pictures, sharing, "We already played and ate dinner, What's next?" She then indicates to Jinho to cross off the restroom reminder that is next in line. Jinho crosses this picture off and puts his pen down.

Meanwhile, his sister goes outside and gets the basketball. Showing it to Jinho, she inquires, "Want to play?" Exhibiting his agreement Jinho flaps his hands with excitement and begins to move towards his sister.

Mom stops the two. "Hold on a minute. Jinho you need to use the restroom first." Holding her phone with a picture of the bathroom in front of his sister's ball. she says purposefully, "First, restroom, then basketball."

Jinho agreeably runs toward the restroom but finds the door closed. He stops and looks back at Mom. Realizing that Dad is using the restroom, Mom approaches Jinho and places his hand on the wall, saying, "wait."

Jinho is well practiced at this direction and stands with his hand on the wall for the next minute while Dad finishes-up. As soon as Dad opens the door, Jinho rushes past, uses the restroom, and washes his hands. While Jinho was in the restroom, his sister was instructed to get a light sweater because it was getting cool outside.

Mom also picked three options for Jinho. As he exited the bathroom, Mom greeted Jinho with the sweaters and said, "Pick one." Jinho grabbed his black sweater, and then responding to his sister's wave to come, he ran outside.

While his sister and he were enjoying their basketball game, Dad came outside. Whistling to get the kids attention Dad holds his hands out in a catching motion encouraging Jinho to pass him the ball. Jinho includes his father in the game, and the three take turns shooting at the basket.

After a while, Dad wants to practice Jinho's Adapted Physical Education (APE) goal to play as a team. Dad begins instructing Jinho and his sister to pass the ball around before shooting into the basket. To help Jinho understand Dad arranges four pictures together on his smart phone. One picture of Jinho's sister, one picture of Dad, one picture of the basket, and one with all three choices. When Jinho has the basketball, Dad shows him a picture indicating where to throw the ball: Dad, sister, basket. Sometimes, Dad would show Jinho the screen with all three pictures allowing him to choose for himself. Jinho always chose to shoot the ball. Dad and the kids had fun playing basketball.

As the evening winds down, the three of them make their way back indoors. Jinho wanders back to the couch where he had been playing on his tablet before dinner. When he is unable to find his tablet, he pulls his Mom by the hand and asks for help. Mom shows Jinho that she had put it away in the locked cabinet. Jinho expresses his disappointment, and Mom recloses and locks the door to indicate her decision is final.

Offering him three pictures of other activities, Mom redirects Jinho to play with something else. Knowing he is unable to influence his mother once she locks the door, Jinho accepts the offer and plays with his cars in the living room.

When bath time arrives, Dad encourages Jinho to clean-up and check his schedule. Jinho puts his toys away and independently goes to his picture schedule hanging in the kitchen.

Accompanying Jinho, Dad crosses off the play picture, stating, "We are done playing; now it's time for…" Pausing to let him respond, Dad waits for Jinho to mark off Shower. Jinho heads into the restroom and disrobes dropping his clothes on the floor.

"Jinho, those go into the hamper."

Flapping his hands and bouncing around the bathroom, Jinho ignores his father's instructions. Shaking the hamper and opening the lid, Dad repeats, "Jinho! Hamper!" The ruckus of the hamper shaking catches Jinho's attention and his Dad's opening the lid spurs Jinho's response. Jinho picks up his dirty clothes and places them in the hamper.

After his shower, Jinho relaxes in his room by spinning his favorite toy. Mom comes into his room and shows Jinho a schedule for the next day. Explaining that tomorrow is Sunday and the family will be going to a birthday party for his cousin after lunch, she shows him a schedule with only seven pictures on it. The simple schedule shows: Get Dressed, Breakfast, Play, Lunch, Party, Shower, Bed. Mom then hangs his picture schedule for the next day's activities in the kitchen, and Jinho goes to sleep.

Discussion

Adding a variety of cues and visual supports to communication facilitates understanding for children with autism. Good understanding increases the speed and competence with which the child is able to respond. Making communication easy through the use of cues and visual supports helps children with autism to cooperate and engage positively with their families. When using visual supports to assist in choice, it is highly recommended to use the most naturally occurring supports available or the highest level of visual support the child can understand consistently. You will see throughout Jinho's evening that his family fluidly utilizes a large variety of cues, visual supports and schedule elements.

Naturally occurring cues and visual supports are often the most accessible and make the most practical options. A good example in Jinho's story is when Mom uses a tactile cue by gently rubbing Jinho's arm to gain his attention as he played on his tablet. Further, she brings a dinner plate with her to let Jinho know it is time to eat. Mom didn't need to find a picture of the dinner table because the plate was right there, naturally available to be used as a cue. Jinho's sister used the basketball to ask him to play with her, and dad used the hamper as a natural cue for Jinho to clean up his clothes.

Gesture and pantomime cues that Jinho knows well were quick and easy supports his family used effortlessly. Mom rubbed her hands together when requesting Jinho wash his hands before dinner. His sister beckoned him outside with a "come here" wave. And, Dad requested to be passed the basketball by moving his hands in a catching motion.

Other cues displayed in Jinho's tale included the auditory cues of Dad whistling to gain his attention on the basketball court, and shaking the hamper in the bathroom. Environmental cues of closed doors let Jinho know he could not access the location or item of his interest. Further, Mom used a tactile, environmental, and verbal cue together when asking Jinho to wait near the bathroom door. She placed his hand on the wall indicating he stand where he was touching the wall while verbalizing the direction, "Wait."

When making requests or offering items that are not immediately available, using the highest level of visual supports the child can consistently understand will be beneficial. Jinho is able to understand pictures on electronic devices. Both his Mom and Dad effectively use these when providing instructions and choices. Jinho also understands that crossing off a picture with a marker indicates that the activity is finished. His picture schedule reflected this skill level. If he needed to take the picture off to show it is gone and no longer accessible, then they would have used this level of support. If Jinho were able to read, then simply writing the words down on a paper or showing words on the phone would be fast and show respect for his skill level.

Helping children to understand the plan of activities throughout the day decreases anxiety and develops coping skills during changes. Using visual schedules even when the day's plan is routine and predictable helps children develop a habit of referencing information about their day. Without other tools, children with autism simply decide how the day's activities should be based on previous experiences. Learning to reference information through visual schedules will benefit the child when new or different activities are planned. In our story, occasionally referencing a simple picture schedule helps Jinho to understand expectations throughout his day, and gives him regular practice with this tool. You will notice that Jinho does not need to reference his schedule for every transition. He is able to cooperatively and naturally transition through a variety of activities without being directed by his schedule. The family assists in identifying and checking off activities that were accomplished without interaction with the list. Mom and Dad only prompt Jinho to his schedule on reminders of using the restroom and taking a shower. Further, Mom used an abbreviated schedule through a first/then visual when reminding Jinho, "First restroom, then basketball." Last, Mom prepared Jinho for changes in the Sunday's schedule by showing him that the family will be attending a party. The Sunday schedule was limited as Jinho only needed support to comprehend the overall plan for the day. He does not need the complete details of each activity. Choosing to use schedules regularly in this less rigid manner allows his family to become comfortable communicating through this support without overwhelming them with more demands on their or Jinho's time and attention.

CHAPTER 7

Conclusion

Has the information presented within this book been informative and helpful? Have you discovered logical and easy ways to implement choice and structured naturally into your interactions with your autistic child? Throughout the book the benefits of offering plentiful structured choices has been demonstrated. May this approach become a habit. Structured Choice is complimented by the addition of just a little organization and planning when supervising unstructured days. To assist in the planning steps, the elements involved in noticing and addressing space, energy and time have been explored. It is my sincere hope that using the strategies discussed in this book will help families to increase positive and productive interactions with their autistic children. Further may the strategies be supportive enough that families find themselves utilizing many of the suggestions for years to come.

Structured Choice

Structured Choice is a powerful strategy to use with autistic children. Incorporating Structured Choice abundantly throughout daily activities will improve engagement and cooperation. For parents, developing a habit of interacting through Structured Choice may take practicing a small mental shift. Focusing on the offering of choices more often than giving instructions, requests, or demands will change the interactions immensely. Threaded through the fabric of this book, you will notice that providing Structured Choice does not take away parental controls, expectations or limits. I propose that when used skillfully, Structured Choice helps parents maintain expectations while preventing protest behaviors. Parents still need to hold firm in their resolve once a decision is made. But, redirecting the children by empowering them with choice will improve the situation immensely.

Plentiful Structured Choice daily improves focused attention, empowerment, and engagement. While implementing Structured Choice, children mentally focus in on accepting an offer. This focus maintains the child's mind-set on the choice. Concentrating on choice prevents the temptation to embark on a yes/no, or accept/reject power struggle. Keeping things light and cooperative is an outcome of Structured Choice.

Offering children with autism many opportunities to make choices supports their basic human need to feel empowered. Each opportunity freely offered provides children a chance to make their wishes known and have those wishes honored. The more frequent the children feel the power of having their expressed wishes satisfied the more self-confident they become. As children become more self-confident, they also become more cooperative. Without a need to fight for a sense of power, children are happier to follow instructions and engage positively with family members. Structured Choice freely offers empowerment and delivers on the offer through immediately producing results. Structured Choice generates engaged interactions and improved relationships.

When using structured choices, remembering the following principles will keep the interactions quick, easy and empowering:

- Offer an abundance of Structured Choice opportunities daily.
- Structured choices need to be things that are relevant to the current, in-the-moment activity.
- Keep the choice sets limited to 2-4 items or activities.
- The child's indicated preference must be honored immediately.
- Limit your words and speak purposefully.
- Use visual supports to enhance understanding and responding.
- Offer choices across a multitude of objects, activities, interests, locations, and desirability levels.
- Allow the child to respond by using the most consistent communication skill they are able to express.

The magic ingredient in Structured Choice is the abundance of choice opportunities offered to the children. Give as many choices as your imagination can muster. Big choices, little choices, important choices, insignificant choices, silly choices, creative choices. Any choice is better than no choice at all.

Satiation & Fixation

Satiation is the act of becoming overly tired of something. Fixation is the experience of becoming overly captivated by something. These two concepts are polar opposites yet yield similar difficulties. Long days at home during holiday weekends and school vacations may result in children with autism becoming less engaged with their toys, more disengaged from their family and exhibiting higher levels of protest behaviors. In order to fight back against the impact of satiation and fixation parents need to find ways to organize materials, and moderate access to toys and activities. This moderation will increase interest and stimulate engagement.

Environmental Structure

When structuring the environment key strategies to consider include:

- Re-assembling and organizing the toys.
- Identifying materials by function of play and areas of play.
- Deciding on zones of play.
- Storing materials in a manner that will support organization, clarity of purpose, ease of use, and smooth transitions.

The Dance

Identifying the variables that impact space, energy and time factors for activities is like bringing together the stage, motion, and timing to perform a beautiful dance. When planning the schedule of the day, it is important to consider the location, movement, and time factors of each activity. When identifying space issues, the type of space, amount of space and function of the space is noted. Looking at energy it is important to understand the movement levels that are inherent within each activity. Planning for variable energy levels throughout the day will support cooperation and engagement. Further, it is beneficial to notice the behaviors that indicate a need for a change in energy before the activity becomes disruptive. The values of time to be considered include the length of activities, the tolerance levels of the child and the global timing needs of all family members. In the interest of moderation, it is suggested to change location, materials, and energy levels regularly throughout the day. It is further suggested that the same activities not be repeated within the identical location, while utilizing the identical materials in any one day. Mix-it-up to keep it fresh and interesting.

Comprehension and Communication

To best achieve comprehension and communication children with autism need multiple and varied amounts of cues and visual supports. These supports benefit receptive and expressive communication skills. The better children with autism understand, the better they respond. Using a variation of cues and visual supports is imperative to reducing anxiety and allowing positive, cooperative interactions. Naturally occurring visual supports are often quick and easy to implement. These include environment, objects, and gestures. Print supports are highly supportive to children with autism. Picture supports are the superstars of visual supports because they are specific, constant and easily portable. Children with autism need clear, concise and purposeful communication.

Cues and visual supports are the aides that best ably meet these needs. Teaching children to reference visual schedules will support their ability to understand the plan of the day. This skill also redirects the child's inclination to decide how the plan should go based solely on previous experience or internalized expectations. Learning to reference schedules helps manage anxiety when the plan changes.

In Closing

In revisiting our tales with Kiaan, Torin, Francesca, Alissa, and Jinho, you will find a wealth of examples with choice and structure being used fluidly by the families portrayed. I encourage you to see if you can identify illustrations of information from each chapter within all of the stories. Do these depictions help you visualize how you might find ways to try organizing your environment, planning your day, and offering more Structured Choices to your child? I hope you visit these stories often for insights, and inspiration of how you can include choice and structure into your daily lives. I wish you much success in supporting your autistic children at home. May your efforts result in increased engagement, improved cooperation and enhanced positive relationships with your children.

References

Bloomfield, B.C. (2001). *Icon to I Can, A Visual Bridge to Independence*. Presentation Materials.

Buck, N. (2013). *How to Be a Great Parent: Understanding Your Child's Wants and Needs.* New York: Beaufort Books.

Burns D. (2008). *Feeling Good: The New Mood Therapy*. New York, Broadway Books.

Frost, L. A., & Bondy, A. S. (1994). *PECS The Picture Exchange Communication System, Training Manual.* New Jersey: Pyramid Educational Consultants, Inc.

Glasser MD, W. (2010). *Choice Theory: A New Psychology of Personal Freedom.* New York: HarperCollins.

Glasser MD, W. (2013). *Take Charge of Your Life: How to Get What You Need with Choice-Theory Psychology.* Indiana: iUniverse.

Lansbury, J. (2014). *Elevating Child Care: A Guide to Respectful Parenting.* JLML Press.

Leaf, R., & McEachin, J. (1999). *A Work in Progress, Behavior Management Strategies and a Curriculum for Intensive Behavioral Treatment of Autism.* New York: DRL Books, L.L.C.

Maurice, C., Green, G., & Luce, S. C. (1996). *Behavioral Intervention for Young Children with Autism, a Manual for*

Parents and Professionals. Texas: Pro-ed, Inc.

McNeil, C. (2017). *Understanding the Challenge of "No" for Children with Autism: Improving Communication, Increasing Positivity, Enhancing Relationships.* Hollister, CA: MSI Press, LLC.

Olver, K. (2019). *Choosing Me Now: Letting Go of What Doesn't Work to Make Room for What Does.* InsideOut Press.

Omer, H. (2011). *The New Authority: Family, School, Community.* New York: Cambridge University Press.

Primason, R. (2004). *Choice Parenting.* New England: iUniverse, Inc.

Steve L. (Presenter). (4/23-26/2002). *TEACCH **T**reatment and **E**ducation of **A**utistic and related **C**ommunication **H**andicapped **Ch**ildren.* Training materials from TEACCH Core Training. Southern California Autism Training Collaborative (SCATC).

ABOUT THIS BOOK

BOOK AWARDS

The first edition of this book has received the following awards:

GOLD AWARD
- Category: Education
- Competition: Reader Views Literary Awards

SILVER AWARD
- Category: Parenting
- Competition: Reader Views Literary Awards

BOOK REVIEWS

The following are sample reviews of the first edition of this book:

Midwest Book Review

Synopsis: *Choice and Structure for Children with Autism: Getting through the Long Days of Quarantine* by Colette McNeil was written specifically for parents caring for an autistic child during this time of pandemic necessitated quarantine.

A compendium of practical commentary and suggestions, *Choice and Structure for Children with Autism: Getting through the Long Days of Quarantine* is essential and helpful reading for any parent who is confronted by such questions as: Are you productively juggling or really struggling? Is your daughter playing throughout your home or staying alone? During interactions, is your son engaged or enraged? Are your toys being enjoyed or does your child get annoyed? After most days do you feel celebrated or devastated?

Choice and Structure for Children with Autism: Getting through the Long Days of Quarantine offers realistic and effective ideas of support in improving focus, engagement, and cooperation. Some strategies shared include ways to offer thoughtfully chosen choice and structure when engaging with autistic children.

Critique: An absolute 'must' as a coping resource for the parent of an autistic children in this pandemic restricted home environment, *Choice and Structure for Children with Autism: Getting through the Long Days of Quarantine* is especially and unreservedly recommended for personal, family, professional, and community library Disability Parenting collections in general, and Autistic Parenting reading lists in particular.

US Review of Books

Book review by Barbara Bamberger Scott

"Autistic children engage best in environments that are highly structured with predictable schedules and a high level of adult guidance."

Author McNeil presents useful guidelines for parents of autistic children to follow in times of quarantine. While typical children may respond more easily to a lack of school attendance, it is far more difficult for autistic children who rely on routine and habit to provide stimulation and satisfaction. Looking at the daily events in four children's lives as examples, the author suggests several approaches to keeping an autistic youngster engaged and contented. One central element is offering choices. The language and the methods used will enhance the child's ability to choose. Appropriate timeframes should be designated for each activity. Toys, exercises, and learning materials should be organized to take place in predetermined spaces. Gradually the child will come to accept and comply with the newly conceived and reliably repeated structures.

McNeil, who has worked with autistic and special needs children for thirty years, asserts that, probably more than others, autistic youngsters can be negatively affected by the need to remain in the same environment for long periods of time due to virus concerns. She recognizes that some of her intelligently considered strategies will cause parents extra effort at first, but the procedures developed will have long-term value. They include such simple but needed techniques as how to present cues for activities—auditory, physical, spatial, or visual—so that the child can quickly grasp and easily remember them. Arranging and offering toys by purpose—artistic, building, watching, moving—will also help the child make choices, as will delineating particular spaces for each activity. The timing for certain activities is helpfully suggested so parents will note when it is best to switch to the next game or task. McNeil's practical and portable volume can be a valuable reference work for parents of autistic children during periods of health restrictions or any similar time.

Readers' Favorite

Reviewed by K. C. Finn

5 stars

Choice and Structure for Children with Autism: Getting Through the Long Days of Quarantine is a work of non-fiction in the parenting, advice, and guidance and supporting text sub-genres, and was penned by author Colette McNeil. As the title suggests, the work is aimed at parents, carers, and guardians of young people who are on the autistic spectrum, and especially homes in on this difficult time of staying at home and changing routines because of worldwide factors beyond our control. As such, the author provides information, guidance, and empathy as you work on improving your child's focus, positive engagement with stimuli, and utilizing co-operation during playtimes.

Author Colette McNeil has provided some invaluable guidance in this well-crafted and jam-packed short guidebook. One of the things which I found especially helpful was its accepting and open tone, which encourages parents not to despair over normal difficulties which are exacerbated when children stay at home. The work is very well structured and organized so that we build upon different basic principles and ideas, leading to an overall enhancement of our understanding of choice and structure, and therefore allowing us as caregivers to deliver much more effective scenarios for children to enjoy their time at home and not get frustrated or upset. What results is a compassionate and useful guide that will provide much-needed help for parents of autistic children, but also the wider spectrum of children with more specific needs. Overall,

I would highly recommend *Choice and Structure for Children with Autism* to those seeking more guidance at this time.

Reviewed by Jamie Michele

5 stars

Choice and Structure for Children with Autism: Getting Through the Long Days of Quarantine by Colette McNeil is a timely non-fiction self-help guide for parents who find themselves at home with children that require a bit more energy and attention than others. McNeil offers readers suggestions on how to best manage the time and specific needs of home-bound children, circumventing issues that may be compounded by the boredom and isolation heightened during the unavoidable quarantine. This is a short but very concise book with coping recommendations ranging from the power of choice, wherein a child is given two or three options for play or stimulation to encourage a sense of agency, alternating options to avoid satiation and fixation, creating structured areas, and learning how to move between them, among other things.

Initially, when I picked up *Choice and Structure for Children with Autism*, I wasn't sure how much information I could really get from a book that is relatively compact. It was an unnecessary thought as Colette McNeil is the consummate pro at delivering the facts without any fluff. It was refreshing to feel like I was chatting with a friend, a narrative style that makes a reader immediately comfortable with the author. I also really liked how after each suggestion was made McNeil gives an example in the form of a story. Even though we all have children that relate in different ways, the similarities were close enough that every single case presented was one I could replicate with immediate effect. As a result, this is the first time I have read a book where I knew the author 'gets me'...or us, as a family. Very highly recommended.

Reviewed by Edith Wairimu

5 stars

Choice and Structure for Children with Autism: Getting Through the Long Days of Quarantine by Colette McNeil is a helpful guide that proposes ways for improving interaction with autistic children, especially during the current season as many families are staying home with limited opportunities to engage their children. While the current quarantine period poses difficulties for all children, McNeil explains that for children with autism, the unstructured environment presents more challenges since autistic children thrive in a highly structured and predictable environment. The work explains how choice and structure can be utilized to enhance productivity and interaction with autistic children. Chapters discuss how choices can be produced by introducing multiple opportunities, boredom, and disengagement in the context of satiation and fixation, the dance between space, energy, and time, and more.

I loved that *Choice and Structure for Children with Autism* by Colette McNeil puts forward simple, available strategies that anyone can utilize. In the sixth chapter, for instance, the work explores the use of visual cues such as printed material or the use of pictures on electronic devices to assist comprehension. Such cues are easily available around the home. The information is also practical and timely, especially during our current times. Each chapter is an in-depth exploration of the topics and stories of common scenarios are included. They are useful in illustrating and explaining the content. In the last chapter, helpful summaries of the chapters are included. They emphasize and bring attention to key information in the book. *Choice and Structure for Children with Autism* by Colette McNeil is an educative and handy guide for parents with autistic children, especially during the quarantine period.

Reader Views

Reviewed by Tammy Ruggles for Reader Views

Choice and Structure for Children with Autism: Getting through the Long Days of Quarantine by Colette McNeil is the perfect little book to help parents of autistic children manage the often-difficult time of quarantine. The author gives valuable insight and advice on how to handle the ups and downs of parenting during quarantine's restrictions.

As McNeil explains, quarantine is hard on everyone, and most families face challenges while living in it, but it can be especially hard for autistic children and their families. All children need structure, of course. This is one of the first things you learn in parenting. But this is true for autistic children as well, if not more so. Autistic children expect and thrive with structure. Without it, they can become overwhelmed, withdrawn, or temperamental. Quarantine is no time to throw routines, patterns, and structure out the window. Choices and structure can actually help your child feel safer, more secure, and happier; with flexibility always being a given. This author is gifted at breaking down recognized and researched therapeutic approaches into everyday parenting practices and communication. Parents will find that choices and structure can improve their own state of mind, lower stress, and create a happier environment for the whole family.

McNeil does a wonderful job of explaining that choice and structure isn't about taking all the fun out of daily life or turning your home into a military operation. It's about creating comfort and routine. Structured Choice is just one example. This is where you limit your child's choices in a strategic way. Example: Giving ALL of the toys at once can be overwhelming. Presenting a few of them (2-4) for him/her to choose from is less overwhelming. Other concepts that the author explains include Focused Attention, Empowerment, Engagement, etc.

What I like about the author's style is that she gets right to the point, right away. Most parents don't have time to fit a super long book of theories and practice into their busy schedule. But this book is laser-focused on each point, offering practical tips based on expert sources that you can start using today with an autistic child. Using anecdotal children like Kiaan, Torin, and others to illustrate the points is a great choice by the author, as most parents and family members can relate to the scenarios. This book is easy to follow; the advice should be easy to implement. *Choice and Structure for Children with Autism: Getting through the Long Days of Quarantine* by Colette McNeil needs to be in the home of every family with an autistic child.

About the Author

Author Biography

Colette McNeil is the author of the award-winning books, *Choice and Structure for Children with Autism: Getting through the Long Days of Quarantine* (MSI Press LLC) and *Understanding the Challenge of "No," for Children with Autism: Improving Communication, Increasing Positivity, Enhancing Relationships* (MSI Press LLC).. A Spanish translation of the latter, is in press, with anticipated publication in late 2022.

With over 30 years of experience working with children with autism in a wide range of educational, recreational, and care giving settings, Colette McNeil holds a master of arts degree in psychology and follows positive psychology inspirations. She aspires to develop confidence in children with autism through expanding the perspectives of their parents, families, teachers, and caregivers.

Colette McNeil has over 70 evidence-based trainings in supporting individuals with autism and developmental disabilities including advance level training in the following evidence-based, autism focused instruction:

- Intensive Behavioral Instruction (IBI) which includes ABA practices.
- PECS - Picture Exchange Communication System

- TEACCH - Treatment and Education of Autistic and related Communication Handicapped
- The SCERTS Model, a Comprehensive Educational Approach for Children with Autism Spectrum Disorder
- ICON to ICAN - Visual Supports
- Links to Language
- Pivotal Response Training

Website:

Shared Perspectives Support

> SPSforAutism.com

> http://sharedperspectivessupport.com/wp-content/uploads/2021/05/Colette-M.jpg

Special Recognition: Top Communication Advisor for *Autism Parenting Magazine*

Top Communication Advisor

COLETTE McNEIL, M Psych

Colette is the author of the award-winning book *Understanding the Challenge of "No," for Children with Autism: Improving Communication, Increasing Positivity, Enhancing Relationships*. She covered the subject of nonverbal communication and personal communication supports for *APM* and is joining the lineup for the next Autism Parenting Summit. Colette has worked with children on the spectrum for 30 years in a range of educational, recreational, and caregiving settings.

🌐 http://spsforautism.com/

f https://www.facebook.com/SPSforAutism/

🐦 https://twitter.com/supportshared

Author's Books

As noted in the author's biography, she has published the following books in paperback, e-book, and hard cover variants:

Choice and Structure for Children with Autism: Getting through the Long Days of Quarantine (MSI Press LLC 2020; first edition of this book, written to assist parents in lockdown from COVID-19 pandemic regulations; as noted above, winner of Gold and Silver Literary Titan awards in the respective categories of education and parenting)

Choice and Structure for Children with Autism: Second Edition (first edition adjusted to post-pandemic "at-home" aspects of successfully parenting children with autism)

Understanding the Challenge of "No" for Children with Autism: Improving Communication, Increasing Positivity, Enhancing Relationships (MSI Press 2020; winner of Kops-Fetherling International Book Awards Competition Legacy Award in Education and Reader Views Literary Awards Silver Award in Classical Adult Nonfiction; ranked as #34 of Bookauthority's 2020 top 74 best Positivity books of all time)

Entienda el desafío del -NO- en los niños con autismo (Spanish-language edition of *Understanding the Challenge of "No" for Children with Autism*; in press).

Author's Publications on the Topic of Autism

In addition to her books on this topic, since February 2018, Colette McNeil has published a number of articles about autism, including selected ones listed below:

Date	Name of Article	Publication Source
4/2022	Creating Choice and Structure at Home	On-Line Presentation Autism Parenting Summit April 2022
9/1/2021	Personal Communication Supports: For Nonverbal Children with Autism	Autism Parenting Magazine Issue 127, Pages 62-65 www.autismparentingmagazine.com
6/27/2021	A Mobile Safe Space	Shared Perspective Support Post www.SPSforAutism.com Facebook + add, Twitter
5/20/2021	Well-Chosen Words	Shared Perspective Support Post www.SPSforAutism.com
2/1/2021	How Counting to Twenty Can Help Your Child with Autism	Autism Parenting Magazine, Issue 118, Pages 59-62. www.autismparentingmagazine.com
10/1/2020	Leading with Choice: Honoring and Empowering Autistic Children	Autism Parenting Magazine Issue 109, Pages 7-9 www.autismparentingmagazine.com
9/7/2020 6/29/2020	Highlighting Choice While Setting Limits	Shared Perspective Support Post www.SPSforAutism.com
8/31/2020	Loose Structure for Long Days of Play	Shared Perspective Support Post www.SPSforAutism.com
7/14/2020	Pantomime, We Do it All the Time	Shared Perspective Support Post www.SPSforAutism.com

5/24/2020	Engaging Autistic Children's Personal Power	Shared Perspective Support Post www.SPSforAutism.com
3/31/2020	Relationships, Autism and "No"	Shared Perspective Support Post www.SPSforAutism.com
11/12/2018	Come Here	Shared Perspective Support Post www.SPSforAutism.com
10/22/2018	Have You Practiced the Halloween Instructions with Your Autistic Children?	Shared Perspective Support Post www.SPSforAutism.com
9/23/2018	New School Year and Your Child with Autism Shared Perspective Support Post	Shared Perspective Support Post www.SPSforAutism.com
8/18/2018	Insights from an Autism Class	Shared Perspective Support Post www.SPSforAutism.com
6/15/2018	Six Suggestions to Manage Summer Changes	Shared Perspective Support Post www.SPSforAutism.com
3/26/2018	What is this Child Trying to Accomplish with This Behavior?	Shared Perspective Support Post www.SPSforAutism.com
4/26/2018	The Platinum Rule	Shared Perspective Support Post www.SPSforAutism.com
2/27/2018	Autism Engagement Tips	Shared Perspective Support Post www.SPSforAutism.com

RELATED MSI PRESS BOOKS

10 Quick Homework Tips (Alder & Trombly)

108 Yoga and Self-Care Practices for Busy Mamas (Gentile)

365 Teacher Secrets for Parents: Fun Ways to Help Your Child in Elementary School (Alder & Trombly)

Andrew's Awesome Adventures with His ADHD Brain (K. Wilcox & A. Wilcox)

Choice and Structure for Children with Autism (McNeil)

Clean Your Plate! 13 Things Good Parents Say That Ruin Kids' Lives (Bayardelle)

Girl, You've Got This! A Fitness Trainer's Personal Strategies for Success Transitioning into Motherhood (Renz)

How to Be a Good Mommy When You're Sick (Graves)

I Love My Kids, But I Don't Always Like Them (Bagdade)

Lamentations of the Heart, Mixed with Joy and Peace (Wells-Smith)

Lessons of Labor: One Woman's Self-Discovery through Birth and Motherhood (Aziz)

Life after Losing a Child (Romer & Young)

Noah's New Puppy (R. Rice, V. Rice, & Henderson)

One Simple Text: The Liz Marks Story (Shaw & Brown)

Parenting in a Pandemic (Bayardelle)

Soccer Is Fun without Parents (Jonas)

Understanding the Analyst (Quinelle)

Understanding the Challenge of "No" for Children with Autism (McNeil)

Understanding the Critic (Quinelle)

Understanding the Entrepreneur (Quinelle)

Understanding the People around You: An Introduction to Socionics (Filatova)

Understanding the Seeker (Quinelle)

Letter to the Reader

Dear Reader,

Thank you for reading Colette McNeil's book on *Choice and Structure for Children with Autism*. Whether you are a parent, relative, or teacher of a child with autism, we hope it has provided you with useful suggestions along with resources for your own work with this challenging but rewarding population. We also hope it has brought you a sense of comfort and peace—that you are not alone and that yes, you can both help and enjoy the child(ren) in your life who has autism.

If you found this book helpful, would you consider writing a book review? You can post it on the site where you bought the book. If you like, you can send it to the publisher at info@msipress.com.

We wish you success, light, and joy in your days head with your very special child(ren).

The Editor

www.ingramcontent.com/pod-product-compliance
Lightning Source LLC
LaVergne TN
LVHW051847080426
835512LV00018B/3110